Tending the Tumlin

by Oshri Liron Hakak

illustrated by Gordon Motsinger

BUTTERFLYON BOOKS

First Edition
Copyright ©2023, by Oshri Liron Hakak and Gordon Motsinger
All Rights Reserved

Tending the Tumlin
Art by Gordon Motsinger and Words by Oshri Liron Hakak

Published by Butterflyon Books
Los Angeles
ISBN 979-8-9868755-3-8

For our families, Luca,
and to anyone whose tummy
needs some comfort.

The Tumlin is an imaginary creature who lives in our tummy...
a TUMmy gremLIN needs care when we don't feel so yummy.

This book is about a Tumlin, a girl, and her pet frog.
We hope you enjoy reading along.

When your stomach's a' mumblin'
take heed the Tumlin!

Meanwhile in her tummy
on the Tumlin's boat...

Sounds and sensations
grumblin` and rumblin`...

In our bellies we feel the whole world a'tumblin'
and a grouchy Tumlin in our tummy
can send us a'stumblin'.

To sooth the little creature
who, turns out, is a teacher,
it helps to tune in to our listening feature.

A gentle hand on the belly...
There you go little felly...

And a deep belly breath says,
"Tumlin, time to rest!"

It's nap time on the banana boat...
OUR CAPTAIN

In times of upset, you might ask the Tumlin to slowly share,
"Will you tell me what's all the fuss about down there?"

TumTV

And little by little the Tumlin may open up,
bit by bit telling you exactly what's up.

Dear Friend,
POST
Disembarking the NMS Royal Banana

Eventually the two of you can feel it out,
and rubbing your belly a bit might soothe the Tumlin's pout.

VITAMINS
Contentment Ramen
CoCo
Trip of
Tummy Town
Tummy Town
Garden
LAZY
NOODLE
RIVER
CALL: VEG-TABL
NOODLE LUNCH
BAN
ANA
BOAT
Crop
Party
SKY
TOURS

Without the Tumlin it would have been easy to ignore.
Now you know to give care to this thing in your core.

You can even smile at the Tumlin and softly say,
"Thanks for pointing out this issue — I had gone astray."

Astray Way
PEACHY PATH
GROCERY
RESTAURANT

And the Tumlin might say, through calming or even a burp,
"All your feelings, pleasant and painful, without question I slurp."

ANXIETY
SADNESS
GRATITUDE
JOY

"So thanks for tending to me and letting go
of stuff like when you forgot your lines in the show..."

The Tumlin also has memories to tend...

"To me your healing is most appealing,
and it's not my goal to send you reeling."

"See, when you're feeling in a nervous kind of way
it's because butterflies in your belly have come out to play.
When I let loose my ginormous butterfly herd
it's just because I need to be heard."

"Rather through ease and comfort in your gut,
I'd prefer you walk life with a happy and humble strut."

Tummy Town
Community
Garden
Hopeful Shoots
Jolly Turnips
PEAce Greens

"Now together, let's make the best of today."
"Thank you," you might smile and say.

Yes, with your friend the trusted Tumlin in your tummy
it works best to be chummy.

So, my friend, I won't go on ramblin'...
When your stomach's a'mumblin,
take heed the Tumlin!

The Bend

<u>One Way You Can Tend the Tumlin</u>

1. Sit in a comfortable place.

2. Close your eyes.

3. Put one or both hands gently on your belly.

4. Smile a little bit, focusing your mind on your belly.

5. Take deep breaths, feeling your belly expand when you breathe in, and feeling it deflate when you breathe out. See how slowly and deeply you can breathe in and out, while letting the rest of your body be still and relaxed. Notice what happens after a few breaths.

Oshri loves to make art, music and books that help people feel better. You can find more of his books on ButterflyonBooks.com, and his art is on Instagram on @oshrihakak.

Gordon Motsinger draws funny creatures that are definitely up to something. You can find these creatures on Instagram @gordon.motsinger.art.

www.ingramcontent.com/pod-product-compliance
Lightning Source LLC
Chambersburg PA
CBRC102036110726
48005CB00009BA/1035